The Seven Wonders of the Ancient World

By

Asad Rasool

Table of Contents:

located in present-day Turkey, was a tomb built for King Mausolus by his wife and sister Artemisia. It was considered one of the Seven Wonders for its architectural beauty and grandeur.

Note: It is important to note that this list was compiled by Antipater of Sidon and it was not the only list of wonders, other lists exist and they could include different constructions.

The Great Pyramid of Giza

The Great Pyramid of Giza, also known as the Pyramid of Khufu or the Pyramid of Cheops, is the oldest and only remaining of the Seven Wonders of the Ancient World. It is located on the Giza Plateau, on the west bank of the Nile River in present-day Egypt. The pyramid was built as a tomb for the ancient Egyptian pharaoh Khufu, who ruled from around 2589 to 2566 BCE. It is considered one of the most impressive architectural and engineering achievements in human history.

The Great Pyramid is the largest of the three pyramids on the Giza Plateau and is believed to have been built over a 20-year period during Khufu's reign. It stands at 147 meters (481 feet) tall and is made of over 2.3 million limestone blocks, each weighing an average of 2.5 tons. The pyramid's base covers an area of 13.1 acres, and its four sides are perfectly aligned with the cardinal points.

The pyramid's internal structure is composed of three main chambers, the Queen's Chamber, the King's Chamber, and the Subterranean Chamber. The King's Chamber is located at the heart of the pyramid and is where the sarcophagus of the pharaoh was placed. The pyramid also has a complex system of corridors and passageways that were designed to protect the pharaoh's body and his treasures from grave robbers.

The exterior of the pyramid was once covered in a layer of fine white limestone, which was believed to have been quarried from the nearby Tura limestone formations. This layer was removed over the centuries to be used in other constructions, revealing the rough limestone core of the pyramid. The pyramid is also surrounded by several smaller pyramids, temples, and funerary complexes, which were built for the pharaoh's queens and other members of the royal family.

The construction of the Great Pyramid is one of the greatest mysteries of ancient history. There are several theories about how the pyramid was built, but the most widely accepted theory is that it was built using a combination of manual labor and simple machines. It is believed that the pyramid was built by a workforce of around 100,000 men, who were divided into gangs of around 20,000 men each. The pyramid was built in steps, with each gang working on a different level of the pyramid at the same time.

The Great Pyramid is also known for its precise engineering and alignment. The pyramid is perfectly aligned with the cardinal points, with an error margin of only 3/60th of a degree. The pyramid's corners are also perfectly aligned, with an error margin of only 8 inches. This level of precision is remarkable considering that the pyramid was built over 4,500 years ago, before the invention of the compass or other modern surveying tools.

The Great Pyramid of Giza continues to be an important historical and cultural site, attracting millions of visitors each year. It is also an important archaeological site, and excavations and studies are still ongoing to uncover more information about the pyramid and the civilization that built it. The pyramid and the other pyramids on the Giza Plateau were declared a UNESCO World Heritage Site in 1979, and are considered some of the most important architectural and engineering achievements in human history.

In conclusion, The Great Pyramid of Giza is an extraordinary architectural and engineering achievement that stands as a testament to the ingenuity and skill of the ancient Egyptians. The pyramid is considered one of the most impressive and important historical sites in the world and continues to fascinate and inspire people to this day. The pyramid is a true wonder of the ancient world, and its existence is a reminder of the incredible achievements that human beings are capable of.

The Hanging Gardens of Babylon

The Hanging Gardens of Babylon were one of the Seven Wonders of the Ancient World, a list of remarkable constructions of classical antiquity. The gardens were located in the ancient city of Babylon, which is now in present-day Iraq. They were built by King Nebuchadnezzar II in the 6th century BCE as a gift to his wife, Amytis of Media, who longed for the green hills of her homeland. The gardens were renowned for their beauty and were considered one of the most impressive feats of engineering in the ancient world.

The Hanging Gardens of Babylon were a series of terraced gardens that were said to have been built on top of a massive stone structure, which may have been a palace or a ziggurat. The gardens were built on several levels and were said to have been planted with a variety of trees, shrubs, and flowers. The gardens were watered by a complex system of irrigation channels and pumps, which brought water from the Euphrates River to the top of the gardens.

The gardens were designed to look like a natural hillside and were said to have been a riot of color, with flowers, shrubs, and trees in bloom. The gardens were also home to a variety of animals, including lions, which were said to have roamed the gardens freely. The gardens were also said to have been home to a variety of exotic plants and trees, including cedars, cypresses, and palm trees.

The Hanging Gardens of Babylon were not only known for their beauty but also for their engineering. The gardens were built on a grand scale, with several levels of terraces, each one higher than the last. The terraces were supported by a complex system of arches and vaults, which were designed to distribute the weight of the gardens evenly across the structure. The gardens were also designed to withstand the harsh desert climate, with features such as shading and cooling systems to keep the plants and animals cool during the hot summer months.

The Hanging Gardens of Babylon were not only an impressive engineering achievement but also an important cultural and historical site. The gardens were considered one of the most beautiful and impressive wonders of the ancient world and were visited by many travelers, scholars, and kings. The gardens were also an important symbol of the power and wealth of the

Babylonian Empire and were considered a symbol of the greatness of King Nebuchadnezzar II.

The exact location of the Hanging Gardens of Babylon is unknown. Some historians believe that the gardens were located in the city of Babylon, while others believe that they were located in the nearby city of Nineveh. The gardens were destroyed by an earthquake in the 1st century BCE and have not been rebuilt. However, the gardens continue to inspire people to this day, and many historians, archaeologists, and engineers continue to study the gardens and try to understand how they were built and how they worked.

In conclusion, The Hanging Gardens of Babylon were one of the Seven Wonders of the Ancient World, an architectural and engineering achievement that stood as a testament to the ingenuity and skill of the ancient Babylonians. The gardens were renowned for their beauty, grandeur and engineering and were considered one of the most impressive feats of engineering in the ancient world. The gardens were destroyed by an earthquake in the 1st century BCE, however, the gardens continue to inspire people to this day, and many historians, archaeologists, and engineers continue to study the gardens and try to understand how they were built and how they worked.

The Temple of Artemis at Ephesus

The Temple of Artemis at Ephesus, also known as the Temple of Diana, was one of the Seven Wonders of the Ancient World. It was located in the city of Ephesus in what is now Turkey, and was dedicated to the goddess Artemis, the goddess of hunting, wild animals, virginity, and childbirth in ancient Greek religion.

The temple was built in the 6th century BCE and was reconstructed several times over the centuries. The most well-known version of the temple was built in the 3rd century BCE and was made of marble and decorated with sculptures and friezes. It stood at over 120 feet tall and was surrounded by a walled courtyard.

The temple was a major religious and cultural center in ancient times, and was also an important center of commerce. Many ancient writers, including Herodotus and Pausanias, wrote about the temple and the city of Ephesus.

The temple was destroyed by fire in 356 BCE by Herostratus and was rebuilt by the order of Alexander the Great. It was then destroyed again in the 3rd century CE by the Goths, and later by the Byzantines. Only foundations and a few sculptures remain today, but the site is still considered an important archaeological site.

The temple was also known for its numerous statues and sculptures. There were many statues of Artemis, as well as statues of other gods and goddesses, animals, and mythical creatures. The temple also featured many friezes and reliefs that depicted scenes from Greek mythology, including the labors of Hercules and the battle between the Amazons and the Athenians.

The temple was also visited by many famous figures in ancient history, including Alexander the Great, who reportedly made offerings at the temple before going to war with the Persians.

The Temple of Artemis at Ephesus was a significant and iconic structure of the ancient world, known for its grandeur, architectural design, and religious and cultural importance. It is considered one of the most important examples of ancient Greek architecture and art and is an important site for the study of ancient history and archaeology.

The Statue of Zeus at Olympia

The Statue of Zeus at Olympia was one of the Seven Wonders of the Ancient World, and was considered one of the greatest masterpieces of ancient Greek sculpture. The statue depicted the god Zeus sitting on a throne, and was made of gold and ivory. It was created by the renowned Greek sculptor Phidias around 435 BCE, and was placed in the Temple of Zeus at Olympia, a sanctuary dedicated to the god located in the western Peloponnese region of Greece.

The statue stood at a staggering 43 feet tall and was made of wood that was covered in gold and ivory plates. The throne was also made of wood and was decorated with gold, ebony, ivory, and precious stones. The statue depicted Zeus in a seated position, wearing a garment made of gold and adorned with precious stones, and holding a scepter in his right hand and a Nike, the goddess of victory, in his left hand. The statue's face and hair were also made of gold and were said to have been so lifelike that it seemed as if Zeus himself had come to life.

The statue was considered a masterpiece of art and craftsmanship, and was greatly admired by the ancient Greeks. Pausanias, a Greek traveler and geographer of the 2nd century CE, wrote that the statue was "a work worthy of gods, and not of men."

The statue was also an important religious and cultural symbol for the ancient Greeks, as Zeus was the king of the gods and the god of thunder and lightning. The statue was located in the Temple of Zeus, where the Olympic Games were held every four years. These games were considered one of the most important religious and athletic events in ancient Greece, and the statue of Zeus was an important part of the experience for the athletes and visitors.

Unfortunately, the statue of Zeus no longer exists today. It was destroyed in the 5th century CE, likely by fire or looting. However, descriptions and depictions of the statue have been passed down through history, and it continues to be remembered as one of the greatest masterpieces of ancient Greek art and craftsmanship.

The Temple of Zeus where the statue was located also no longer exists, but the ruins of the temple have been excavated and studied by archaeologists. The site of the temple is now a UNESCO World Heritage Site, and the remaining architectural elements, such as the altar and the stadium, continue to be an important testimony of the religious and cultural significance of ancient Olympia.

The statue of Zeus at Olympia was a towering masterpiece of ancient Greek sculpture, and its influence can still be seen in art and architecture today. It was a testament to the skill and creativity of the ancient Greek artists, and a symbol of the religious and cultural importance of the god Zeus and the Olympic Games in ancient Greece. It continues to be remembered and admired as one of the Seven Wonders of the Ancient World.

The Colossus of Rhodes

The Colossus of Rhodes was a statue of the Greek god Helios, built in 280 BC on the island of Rhodes, Greece. It was one of the Seven Wonders of the Ancient World, and stood at over 100 feet tall, making it one of the tallest statues of the ancient world. The statue was built to celebrate Rhodes' victory over the ruler of Cyprus, Antigonus I Monophthalmus, who had besieged the island in 305 BC.

The Colossus was constructed by the sculptor Chares of Lindos, and was made of bronze plates that were fastened to an iron framework. The statue stood at the entrance of the harbor of Rhodes, and was said to be so large that ships could sail between its legs. The statue was said to have been so impressive that it was said to "shine with the radiance of the sun" and was visible from far out at sea.

The Colossus stood for only 56 years before it was destroyed by an earthquake in 226 BC. The statue was so large that it took more than 800 years for the pieces to be removed. The remains of the statue were then sold to a Jewish merchant, who is said to have sold the metal to a scrap metal dealer.

The Colossus of Rhodes was an important symbol of the city of Rhodes and its powerful naval presence in the Mediterranean. It also served as an inspiration for many other statues and monuments throughout history, including the Statue of Liberty in New York City. Today, the Colossus of Rhodes is remembered as one of the most impressive and iconic statues of the ancient world, and its legacy continues to inspire people around the world.

The Lighthouse at Alexandria

The Lighthouse at Alexandria, also known as the Pharos of Alexandria, was a towering structure built on the island of Pharos in the harbor of Alexandria, Egypt. It is considered one of the Seven Wonders of the Ancient World.

Construction of the lighthouse began during the reign of Ptolemy II Philadelphus in the 3rd century BC and was completed around 280 BC. The lighthouse was made of marble and stood at an impressive height of around 394 feet (120 meters), making it one of the tallest structures in the world at the time.

The lighthouse served as a guide for ships entering the harbor of Alexandria, and its light was produced by a fire that was kept burning at the top of the structure. The fire was used to reflect sunlight during the day, and at night, a mirror was used to reflect the light of the fire.

The lighthouse also served as a landmark for the city of Alexandria, and it was said that its light could be seen from as far away as 35 miles (56 kilometers). The lighthouse was also used as a navigational aid for ships entering the harbor of Alexandria, and its light helped to guide ships safely to port.

The lighthouse was also an architectural marvel, with a spiral ramp leading to the top of the structure, allowing visitors to ascend to the top. The structure also featured a large statue of Poseidon at the entrance, and a temple dedicated to the god at the top.

The lighthouse stood for over 1,500 years, surviving earthquakes and other natural disasters. However, it was eventually destroyed by a series of earthquakes in the 14th century AD, and only ruins of the lighthouse remain today.

Despite its destruction, the lighthouse at Alexandria continues to be celebrated as a symbol of the engineering and architectural achievements of the ancient world. Its legacy lives on in the modern use of lighthouses as navigational aids and in the many architectural structures that have been inspired by it.

The Lighthouse of Alexandria was a technological wonder of its time, and it's one of the most important landmarks of the ancient world. Despite its destruction, it continues to be celebrated as a symbol of the engineering and architectural achievements of the past and a reminder of the power of human ingenuity and creativity.

The Mausoleum at Halicarnassus

The Mausoleum at Halicarnassus was a tomb built during the 4th century BC in the city of Halicarnassus, which was located in what is now modern-day Turkey. It was built as a tomb for Mausolus, the satrap (or governor) of the Persian province of Caria, and his wife, Artemisia II of Caria. The building was considered one of the Seven Wonders of the Ancient World and was one of the most impressive architectural achievements of the time.

The Mausoleum was designed by the Greek architects Satyros and Pythius and was built on a hill overlooking the city. It was a massive structure, measuring approximately 135 feet (41 meters) in height. The tomb was made of white marble and was adorned with a variety of sculptures and reliefs. The most striking feature of the tomb was its ornate façade, which was adorned with 36 columns and a frieze depicting a battle between the Greeks and the Amazons.

The Mausoleum was also adorned with a number of other sculptures and reliefs, including statues of lions and sphinxes, as well as a statue of Mausolus and Artemisia themselves. The statues were made of white marble and were considered to be some of the finest examples of Hellenistic sculpture.

The top of the tomb was a stepped pyramid, topped by a statue of a chariot, driven by four horses and containing statues of the deceased, Mausolus and Artemisia. This statue is known as the "Mausoleum at Halicarnassus, the memory of which was so enduring that the word "mausoleum" was derived from the name of the tomb.

The Mausoleum at Halicarnassus was not only an architectural masterpiece but also a symbol of the power and wealth of the ruler, Mausolus, who was able to commission such an extravagant tomb for himself and his wife. It also served as an inspiration for many other tombs and monuments throughout the ancient world, including the tomb of Alexander the Great in Alexandria.

The Mausoleum at Halicarnassus stood for nearly 17 centuries but was destroyed by various earthquakes and looting. The remains of the tomb were rediscovered in the early 19th century, and many of the sculptures and reliefs have been removed and are now housed in museums around the world. While much of the original tomb has been lost, the memory of the Mausoleum at Halicarnassus lives on as one of the Seven Wonders of the Ancient World and a symbol of the architectural and artistic achievements of the ancient world.

www.ingramcontent.com/pod-product-compliance
Lightning Source LLC
LaVergne TN
LVHW052043160826
845678LV00016B/3601